HAL•LEONARD
INSTRUMENTAL PLAY-ALONG

AUDIO ACCESS INCLUDED

PLAYBACK+
Speed • Pitch • Balance • Loop

VIOLA

THE VERY BEST OF

BACH

To access audio visit:
www.halleonard.com/mylibrary

Enter Code
1167-9222-7839-3532

T0056595

ISBN 978-1-4950-9085-1

HAL•LEONARD®

7777 W. BLUEMOUND RD. P.O. BOX 13819 MILWAUKEE, WI 53213

In Australia Contact:
Hal Leonard Australia Pty. Ltd.
4 Lentara Court
Cheltenham, Victoria, 3192 Australia
Email: ausadmin@halleonard.com.au

Visit Hal Leonard Online at
www.halleonard.com

ADAGIO
from OBOE CONCERTO IN F MINOR
BWV 1059

By JOHANN SEBASTIAN BACH

VIOLA

AIR

from ORCHESTRAL SUITE NO. 3
BWV 1068

By JOHANN SEBASTIAN BACH

VIOLA

Slowly and expressively

Harpsichord

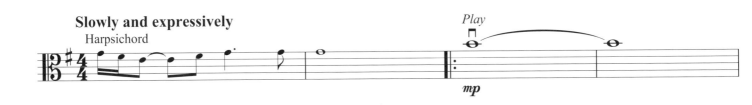

BIST DU BEI MIR

from NOTEBOOK FOR ANNA MAGDALENA BACH

BWV 508

By GOTTFRIED HEINRICH STÖLZEL

VIOLA

BOURRÉE IN E MINOR

from SUITE IN E MINOR FOR LUTE
BWV 996

By JOHANN SEBASTIAN BACH

VIOLA

INVENTION NO. 4
BWV 775

VIOLA

By JOHANN SEBASTIAN BACH

INVENTION NO. 14

BWV 785

By JOHANN SEBASTIAN BACH

VIOLA

JESU, JOY OF MAN'S DESIRING

from CANTATA 147
BWV 147

VIOLA

By JOHANN SEBASTIAN BACH

MINUET
from NOTEBOOK FOR ANNA MAGDALENA BACH
BWV Anh. 116

Composer Unknown

VIOLA

MINUET IN G MAJOR
from NOTEBOOK FOR ANNA MAGDALENA BACH
BWV Anh. 114

VIOLA

By CHRISTIAN PETZOLD

MINUET IN G MINOR

from NOTEBOOK FOR ANNA MAGDALENA BACH

BWV Anh. 115

By CHRISTIAN PETZOLD

VIOLA

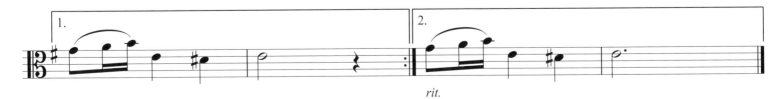

MUSETTE
from NOTEBOOK FOR ANNA MAGDALENA BACH
BWV Anh. 126

VIOLA

Composer Unknown

POLONAISE IN G MINOR
from NOTEBOOK FOR ANNA MAGDALENA BACH
BWV Anh. 119

Composer Unknown

VIOLA

SHEEP MAY SAFELY GRAZE

from CANTATA 208
BWV 208

By JOHANN SEBASTIAN BACH

VIOLA

SICILIANO
from FLUTE SONATA IN E-FLAT MAJOR
BWV 1031

By JOHANN SEBASTIAN BACH

VIOLA

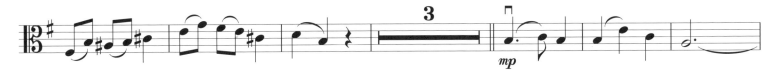

SLEEPERS, AWAKE
(Wachet Auf)
from CANTATA 140
BWV 140

VIOLA

By JOHANN SEBASTIAN BACH